Celebrating Home

DECORATING FOR THE HOLIDAYS AND SEASONS

Celebrating Home

DECORATING FOR THE HOLIDAYS AND SEASONS

from the creative team at

seasons®
of cannon falls

Inspiring Traditions

Foreword by Nancy Mernit Soriano, Editor-in-Chief, *Country Living* magazine

FOREWORD BY
NANCY MERNIT SORIANO 6

INTRODUCTION 8

12

SPRING

SUGAR COOKIES

FRESH WINDOW TREATMENTS

EASTER BASKETS

EASTER EGGS

MOTHER'S DAY

ELEGANT SLIPCOVERS

44

SUMMER

SUMMER BERRIES

GIFTS OF THE SEASON

SUMMER SOLSTICE

WEEKEND GETAWAY

FOURTH OF JULY

PARADES

74

FALL

PRESERVING LEAVES

HALLOWEEN

PUMPKIN CARVING

TRICK OR TREAT

CHILD'S THANKSGIVING

SEASONAL CORNUCOPIA

106

WINTER

CHRISTMAS WELCOME

GIFT GIVING

TREE TRIMMING

CHRISTMAS STOCKINGS

NEW YEAR'S EVE

VALENTINE'S DAY

CREDITS 143

Foreword

One of the greatest joys of publishing *Country Living* is the opportunity it allows us to seek out the creative forces that help shape our homes and our lives. We're always looking for the alchemists among us—those people with a talent for creating something original, beautiful, or extraordinary.

Over the years, our magazine has visited many small towns, including Cannon Falls, Minnesota, where a company with such a talent thrives. Midwest, a home-grown but nationally known holiday and seasonal home accent company, has been an inspiration to us and to our readers. But what we love most about the creative team behind the company's Seasons of Cannon Falls brand is their passion and dedication to the importance of home and the traditions celebrated there.

We've found a kindred spirit in Seasons of Cannon Falls, and we're proud to have featured it, including the River House, in the pages of *Country Living*. That's why I believe you'll enjoy *Celebrating Home*—a book that speaks to decorating ideas centered around home and family, and the traditions celebrated throughout the seasons.

Nancy Mernit Soriano
Editor-in-Chief, *Country Living*

The River House, around the 1890s.

Introduction

This book is dedicated to our founding families, the Althoffs and Brekkens. The spirit of home and love of family traditions that inspired them is alive and well today at Midwest.

Our small town of Cannon Falls is a picture-postcard setting for a company that is truly an American story. Nestled along the banks of the Cannon River, Cannon Falls has a wealth of history intact with more than 29 buildings listed on the National Register of Historic Places. This quintessential American town, located in the heart of Minnesota, is the home of our company and of our founding family, hardworking entrepreneurs who started with nothing more than an idea and a vision.

Begun in 1953 by Ken Althoff, Midwest brought the magic and beauty of German nutcrackers and European handcrafted Christmas ornaments to shops and retailers across the United States. His daughter, Kathy Brekken, carried on the family's entrepreneurial tradition when she became president in 1985.

The Seasons of Cannon Falls River House as it is today.

Under Kathy's leadership, Midwest flourished, becoming one of the leading holiday and seasonal accent companies in the country. The values and operating principles fostered by our founders still guide Midwest today: "Be honest and fair, value home and family."

As I reflect on these enduring values, I am looking out of my window at River House, the historic home that symbolizes the past and future of our company. Built in 1868 by Benjamin Van Campen, a respected business and community leader, the Italianate-style home is one of the oldest and grandest in Cannon Falls. Over time, the house had fallen into a state of profound neglect and was scheduled for demolition unless it could be moved from its original location. At Midwest, we saw this as a unique opportunity to save part of the proud history of Cannon Falls while celebrating the beauty of the past.

On a snowy February night in 2002, we carefully moved the house through the streets of Cannon Falls to the scenic setting where our company's headquarters are located.

Lovingly renovated by a team of architects, builders, and artisans, it was renamed "River House." In its new life, it has become a living showcase for our Seasons of Cannon Falls product line. Through River House, we have found the perfect symbol for the warmth of home. A place for gathering and celebrating traditions. A place that captures the spirit of home and family. It is an ongoing source of inspiration for our designers and artists as we create holiday and seasonal decorations for the home. We hope that our ornaments and unique decorations will inspire and empower you to make the most of family holidays and traditions, creating moments that will be remembered for many years to come.

Our restoration of River House and all that it stands for is also the inspiration behind this book, *Celebrating Home.* In the pages that follow, we offer you a range of ideas for decorating your home and celebrating traditions with your family through-out the seasons, amid the beauty and backdrop of River House. We welcome you to make these ideas your own and to share and celebrate them with your family in your home.

We hope that the products and ideas we share with you will, like River House, retain the timeless virtues of charm, comfort, and celebration. From our founding family to yours, we send our warmest wishes for many happy celebrations at home.

Jeff Wilson

Jeff Wilson, President, Midwest

SUGAR COOKIES   FRESH WINDOW TREATMENTS

EASTER BASKETS   EASTER EGGS

MOTHER'S DAY   ELEGANT SLIPCOVERS

Blossom by blossom, spring begins. A single crocus pushes through sun-warmed soil. Beautiful yellow trumpets bloom along arched branches of forsythia. Hard-frost nights still nip, but the days are gradually getting warmer. Winter's grip can be strong, but time—always—is on spring's side.

Of all the seasons, spring can be the most fickle. We can never predict when it will arrive, but there's no mistaking it when it does. We wake one morning to find that the sunlight has

changed. Intense but kindly, it saturates our winter-weary homes—seeping through curtains, washing over walls. Outside, spring is literally in the air. The underlying chill has lifted and the scent of daffodils and hyacinths floats on the breeze.

At Seasons of Cannon Falls River House, as in many homes across the country, nature's reappearing act inspires us to reawaken and refresh our surroundings. Pull back the curtains. Push open the windows. Let sunlight and the mild breeze sweep into every room.

Few activities match the satisfaction of a spring Saturday spent cleaning floors, washing windows, and banishing dust from nooks and crannies. At the same time, the garden calls. Each warming day brings us closer to the time when we can set out seedlings and move our lives outdoors again.

Spring is a season of possibility and promise. With the fresh air comes clarity and inspiration. Spring cleaning can be the perfect opportunity to reimagine rooms, to rehang pictures and mirrors in new arrangements; change pillow covers and replace heavy winter bedspreads with something lighter and more colorful.

Air out your furnishings on the lawn and, while the neighbors wonder what you're up to, look at rooms in a new light, as if for the first time. Spring madness? Perhaps, but indulge yourself. Bring the pieces back in one by one—starting with what you love the most. Make it the focal point and work around it. Even if you put most of the furniture back the same way, what you do change might make a world of difference. Decorate not only with the things you love, but also with space and light. It's spring—and anything is possible. 🌿

Winter's over and the fire's out at Seasons of Cannon Falls River House, but this hearth and mantelpiece still radiate warmth. Fireplaces don't have to be reduced to set pieces in warmer weather. Consider filling the hearth with an eclectic arrangement of votives and candles or a sturdy glass urn filled with white fairy lights. For a cleaner look, cover the fireplace with an antique, iron fire screen.

Sweep stray pine needles off the mantel and create a spring tableau. Here, a range of white pottery and crystal perfectly matches the neutral tones of freshly picked flowers. A cluster of hyacinths from the garden gives the room a splash of saturated color and a fragrant focal point.

A grouping of botanical prints taken from an old book captures the spirit of the season in a comfortable blend of formal and casual. Using identical frames arranged in a grid extends the vertical lines of the fireplace to raise the eye and acts as an ordered contrast to the easygoing, meadow-picked look of the flowers.

PAPER SHADES Stripped nearly bare to admit spring light, windows can get a quick and clever adornment with handmade shades cut from plain kraft paper. Punch holes along the edges to let sunlight squeeze through, and tie on beaded tassels for sparkle. In place of the scalloped edge here, consider using pinking shears to create a zigzag trim or gluing a grosgrain ribbon along a straight edge for a more tailored look.

With a white backdrop and open shelves as a stage, it's easy to paint a different scene for every season. For spring, introduce colors through mixed vintage wares: Depression glass, painted florals, tin TV trays, and Bakelite flatware.

Keep the spring kitchen airy, light, and clean. Easter eggs perched among herbs on the windowsill and nestled in a tinted glass cookie jar hint at the holiday just around the corner. Countertops that will soon brim with bowls of summer fruits sit now in anticipation of warmer days ahead and the season's first pitcher of fresh-squeezed lemonade.

SUGAR COOKIES Dressed in pastel shades of spring, a stack of buttery sugar cookies is one of those treats that knows no age limits. Try using flower-shape cookie cutters or cut designs freehand. After baking, create your own decorations with colored royal icing, using a pastry bag to add stripes, dots, or even the initials of lucky recipients. Finish off with silver dragées, sprinkles, or colored decorating sugars. For a magical "stained glass" cookie, cut a hole in the center of the dough before baking and fill with a Lifesaver candy (but protect your pans first by lining them with parchment paper).

WHIMSICAL PAINTING on a window—the more naive, the better—can replace curtains in the kitchen this season. A child's acrylic paints are ideal, but any water-soluble paint will work. If you're not comfortable working freehand, consider using a paper stencil. When the season—or your mood—changes, the design can be easily removed with a little soap and water.

THE SPRING KITCHEN

The
Dance
of Light

Whether hung on a simple iron rod or an easy-opening swing arm, linen or cotton panels don't block the light—they welcome it. Light, sheer fabrics, such as organdy, linen, and chiffon are perfect for spring's soft sunlight and gentle breezes, shimmying in the slightest current. These gauzy fabrics allow light to flood into a room while still offering some privacy. Cotton organdy panels are kept flat and neat by hinged rods threaded through the upper and lower hems, right. Small weights or pennies sewn into the bottom hem will keep light, unlined fabrics neatly draped.

Is it so small a thing To have enjoy'd the sun, To have lived light in the spring, To have loved, to have thought, to have done...
—Matthew Arnold

Pale yellow grosgrain ribbon provides just a touch of contrast to pleated linen curtains. Vintage buttons decorate the base of each pleat and provide a handy hanging spot for ornaments at Christmas or year-round. For smaller windows, vintage linen or cotton hand towels make simple, no-sew curtains. Use small curtain clips or wooden clothespins to hang panels from cord stretched across the window. Hang curtains across just the lower half of the window to allow more light in and still have some privacy.

Like a fresh bouquet on a beautifully set table, Easter reigns as the spirited centerpiece of spring.

Easter retains an old-fashioned charm—a sense of honesty and simplicity that echoes the spirit of the season. It is a holiday that usually finds families at home—relaxed, content, and energized by the warming days.

There's undeniable excitement, too—especially for children. While visions of chocolate bunnies dance in their heads, they

EASTER

eagerly shed sweaters and coats and dash across the greening lawns.

Easter visitors and open houses provide great motivation to revitalize our homes. Fresh flowers on the table, fresh color on the walls, even fresh mulch for the garden all contribute to a renewed perspective on life after winter's long slog. Spring promises a world reborn . . . and Easter delivers it.

Sweet dreams are guaranteed beneath a homemade Easter tree. But be prepared to replace the gumdrop buds daily! Refresh the room with linens in bright seasonal colors.

Keep the mood light by finding new uses for old things. Discarded shutters are reborn as bulletin boards—perfect for displaying artwork or even a fine Easter outfit. Here, a string of decorative lights has been used to add sparkle to a window.

Vintage-look storage jars now show off prized collections or other treasures too pretty to be buried in a toy box.

Kids are notorious for losing track of their things. Backpacks, teddy bears, shoes . . . you never know where they'll turn up. But on Easter morning, there's simply no separating a child from their Easter basket.

Easter baskets most likely began with Christian custom when breads, cheeses, and other foods for Easter dinner were taken to morning Mass to be blessed. Over time, baskets were filled with dyed eggs, chocolates, and treats of all kinds.

Traditional baskets were made of woven reed or wicker, then painted or adorned with ribbon. Feel free to be creative in your interpretation. With enough embellishments, such as fresh or fabric flowers, beads and glitter, any plain basket can become a worthy nest for Easter treasures. The contents also can be varied. For those wishing to limit sugar intake, consider zoo or circus tickets or small toys as basket fillers.

Don't forget . . . Easter baskets aren't only for kids. With a glue gun and a little imagination, a wooden crate, a flower pot, or even a Chinese take-out container can become a unique and charming reinterpretation of the classic basket for an older child or adult.

When guests are coming over, replace the winter wreath with a spring posy as a welcome on the door. ✒ The possibilities are abundant as flower beds erupt in color. And if the ideal spring flowers aren't available, why not make your own? Homemade blossoms are easily assembled from crepe or tissue paper, a few beads, and a bit of wire. It's the perfect project for a rainy spring morning. ✒ If your posy is too large or unruly to tie to the handle, consider attaching it to a colored ribbon draped over the top of the door. ✒ Or, for an Easter open house, there's no more appropriate welcome than a cheerful bunny silhouette.

The flowers of late winter and early spring occupy places in our hearts well out of proportion to their size.
—Gertrude S. Wister

Spring Celebration

Brunch is served. An unhurried and elegant spring brunch is one of the true pleasures of this time of year at River House. The occasion may be a bridal shower, Mother's Day, Easter, or simply a get-together of friends and neighbors to celebrate the new season.

Although the occasion calls for fine china, the mood is light and informal. Playful icons of the season—bunnies, lambs, and chicks—roam among the place settings, and a grass centerpiece captures the thrill of the egg hunt in miniature. Floral patterns appear on pillow covers and on the vintage tray and plates displayed around the walls. Peonies add a blush of pink to the table and scent the air with their delicate perfume…the essence of spring.

The table in spring should be a cheerful mix of contrasts and embellishments. Jellybeans tucked in a crystal chandelier brighten the room with the perfect blend of elegance and whimsy. Beaded floral napkin rings effortlessly pull vintage china into the present, and a tiered server mixes rustic with refined.

Fancy bonnets were once required apparel for an Easter parade or the walk to church on Easter Sunday. You can bring back the charm of Easters past by hosting your own family bonnet bee. Invite older relatives to shower the young with stories of grand parades from long ago. While chatting, busy hands (young and old) can transform plain straw hats into expressive personal statements. It's the perfect way to enjoy spring's gentle "front porch" weather... and a great excuse for throwing a girls-only party.

EASTER BONNETS For a crown worthy of the occasion, be whimsical in your design and use an assortment of trimmings. Try showy, compact blossoms from the garden, costume jewelry, ornaments, or even favorite photographs, along with buttons, baubles, ribbons, and bows. Think of your bonnet as a three-dimensional scrapbook. Its fashion lifespan will be short, so go all out to make it memorable.

Simple. Honest. Pure.
The humble egg is nature's perfect package—and the perfect symbol of the arrival of spring and Easter's renewal.

Even in ancient societies, eggs were dyed, decorated, and exchanged as gifts in spring. Among the very wealthy, a favorite technique was gold leafing, but for most people, the process probably wasn't that different from today's. Eggs are colored by boiling them in a wrapping of flower petals or leaves (onion skins are most reliable), or cooked eggs are dipped in a colored solution.

Kids love the messy, magical tradition of egg dying, but why should they have all the fun? Bring out the glitter, glue, paints, and buttons, and pull up your own chair to the table. Take your time and experiment on these fragile (but, thankfully, affordable) "canvases." Eggs aren't just to *be* decorated—try decorating *with* them. Nest them on window ledges, arrange them with flowers in a centerpiece, or use glitter and simple white eggcups to create beautiful initialed "place cards" for the table.

The front hall or foyer of a home is the first room guests see but is often decorated as an afterthought. Think of this high-traffic place as a staging area and treat it to a seasonal updating. It's easy to pull a quick change in a small space like this. By midspring, it's usually safe to move boots and mittens out and dedicate this welcoming spot to seasonal décor. Greet guests (and yourself) with fragrant flowers of the season, a springtime feather tree, a string of colorful paper lanterns, even a vintage wicker basket filled with all the elements for an impromptu picnic. Keep your opening scene light and spontaneous. After all, spring is all about acting on impulse.

Decorating a tree with seasonal ornaments and embellishments is too much fun to do just once a year. When trees are only just coming into bloom, putting a feather tree just inside the front door brings a dash of color to the foyer. As Easter passes, keep the look current by replacing bunnies and eggs with birds, flowers, feathers, and all things springlike.

SPRING GREETINGS

Tissue paper flowers, breakfast in bed, a crayon-scribbled card that says "I Love You, Mom"…the traditions of Mother's Day are all the more meaningful for their sincerity and simplicity.

Mother's Day was established as a national holiday in 1914 as the result of one woman's relentless lobbying. To honor the memory of her own mother, in 1905 Philadelphian Anna M. Jarvis led the effort to get the holiday adopted, first by her home state and ultimately by the entire country.

Observed each year on the second Sunday in May, Mother's Day couldn't be better timed. Spring is in full flower. The soggy stretches of April have given way to longer, warmer days that seem saturated in sunshine. While summer may still officially be several weeks off, in many families this day marks the beginning of the outdoor season—a perfect occasion for dad to fire up the grill and for kids to lavish mom with homemade cards, a tall glass of iced tea, a daisy crown, and a little well-deserved leisure time. All hail the queen, and long may she reign.

Luminous and spirited, the bedroom in spring should delight the senses: This means replacing the cozy retreat of winter with a mood of refreshing calm. Dress the bed with lighter coverings in soft colors; set out floral-patterned linens. Look for alternatives to overhead lights: an antique reading lamp at the bedside, a cluster of votives on the bureau—or add a touch of whimsy with a string of electric blooms tumbling from a vase or paper cone. Small embellishments— such as a beaded May Day basket and a bird silhouette hung from a ribbon—serve to reflect the season.

Using slipcovers is a time-honored means of bringing a fresh look to rooms in spring. Their loose, unfitted nature makes them refreshingly forgiving to work with. With basic sewing skills and inexpensive organdy or muslin, you can make even estate-sale "orphans" part of a well-dressed family. 🌿 For these chairs, the patterns were made simply by pinning the muslin in place and cutting the fabric right on the chair. 🌿 In place of piping, seams were edged with a simple, tidy flange. This keeps the pleated skirt material hanging nicely without appearing overly stiff. 🌿 Grosgrain ribbons make graceful, effortless tiebacks.

May and June... cool, misty mornings gently burned away with a warming spring sun, followed by breezy afternoons and chilly nights.

—Peter Loewer

Sunlight and Shadow

SUMMER BERRIES

GIFTS OF THE SEASON

SUMMER SOLSTICE

WEEKEND GETAWAY

FOURTH OF JULY PARADES

Summer carries with it a pace, a flavor, and an ease all its own. It moves to a soundtrack of outdoor living—whirring lawn sprinklers, chirping cicadas, chimes from the ice cream truck, singing birds, and of course, laughing, carefree children. In homes with kids, traffic never seems to stop. In for a drink, out for a bike ride. In for a snack, out for a run through the sprinkler. In—with grass clippings clinging to wet feet—for a quick dinner, out to chase fireflies…Summer seen through the

SUMMER

eyes of a child is an endless expanse of glorious blank space, a view that adults are no longer privileged to see. But, ah, we have our pleasures, too. The foods of summer arrive in delectable waves…sweet peas and spinach, cherries and strawberries, green beans and tomatoes…one after another they fill market bins (or, if we have a green thumb, our own gardens).

Like most homes, with the coming of summer the very atmosphere at River House is lightened, in fact and in spirit.

The frenzy of spring—filled with cleaning, organizing, and planting, taking up every minute of the too-short days—gives way to a certain sense of ease. The days grow longer, and suddenly we realize there is time enough. We become less concerned with housekeeping and more attuned to enjoying our homes, yards, and gardens. Summer is the time for easy, outdoor living. It's a time of hammocks, picnics, pool and beach days, lemonade and long, hot afternoons.

We celebrate summer in simple ways: casual gatherings with the neighbors on the front porch, leisurely meals built around fresh ingredients, chalk greetings on the sidewalk, and games of freeze tag on the lawn. Summer, it always turns out, is shorter than it seemed in June, sweeter than seems possible, and steeped in memory like no other season. Like a long-forgotten voice from childhood, summer asks nothing more of us than to come out and play.

THE SUMMER KITCHEN

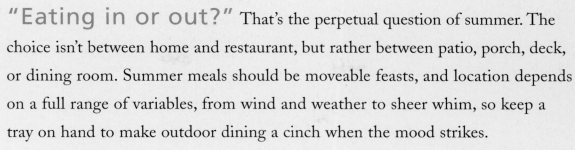

"Eating in or out?" That's the perpetual question of summer. The choice isn't between home and restaurant, but rather between patio, porch, deck, or dining room. Summer meals should be moveable feasts, and location depends on a full range of variables, from wind and weather to sheer whim, so keep a tray on hand to make outdoor dining a cinch when the mood strikes.

Much of the charm of summer meals is their casual style: fresh ingredients simply prepared with little time in the kitchen; a centerpiece of just-picked flowers or berries; a tablecloth as simple as plain brown kraft paper.

Its French doors open to the breeze, the summer kitchen at River House has been pared down to essentials—surfaces have been cleared, ornaments put away. Dashes of red introduced in fabrics echo the color of early summer strawberries and are the perfect accent to the room's cool look. And when it's just too nice to eat indoors, a striped throw on the sofa makes a perfect stand-in picnic blanket.

THE FABRIC OF SUMMER If summer had an official fabric, what else would it be but red gingham? To dress the chairs for the season, use the pattern of picnics to keep the look casual and cool. And it wears well, taking everything from kids in wet bathing suits to runaway berries in its stride. Although summer calls for keeping things simple, there's always room for small embellishments. Sew a scrap of rickrack in a circle and top it with a decorative button to create a miniature gerbera daisy. Add a concealed snap to hold the ribbon tie in place.

There's simply nothing better than fresh summer berries—so why bother trying? "In summer," the poet William Carlos Williams said, "the song sings itself." Likewise, the best summer dishes practically prepare themselves. Even some of the most bruised and squashed berries look like little jewels on a bed of cream.

BERRIED TREASURES Nothing stops the car faster than a roadside stand with a sign that reads Fresh Berries. Berry-picking seasons can be short, so don't miss an opportunity to incorporate these little gems into every meal...or snack! If pies or tarts are too ambitious, fruit salads, the simpler the better, let the flavors of fresh berries star, and berries are also perfect on shortcake or as a topping for yogurt, ice cream, or pancakes. Store-bought pound cake or angel food cake becomes a seasonal delicacy fit for a birthday or summer party when topped with fresh berries and plenty of cream. For a more adult treat, marinate your favorite berries in Grand Marnier, kir, or a similar liqueur with a sprig or two of mint before serving them.

Good cooks follow where fresh ingredients lead—and in summer, the parade of fresh goodies doesn't let up. In turn, the season's fruits and flowers inspire the cheery color palette of the summer kitchen. Prized glassware and china, finds from a yard sale, offer a simple way to add splashes of bold color to the countertops.

Change out or add simple curtains made from kitchen towels, continuing the red theme in ribbon loops and rickrack trim. For more summer color, create a playful backsplash with a line of plates inspired by the summer garden.

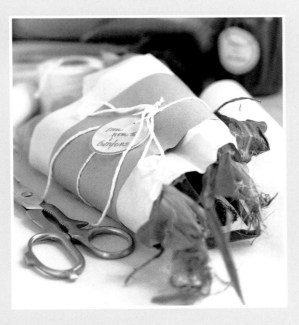

GIFTS OF THE SEASON To arrive at a summer dinner party with an armload of homegrown vegetables and a posy of garden flowers is truly to arrive in style. Summer's rules of engagement are simple. Eat what you can and share the rest. (And if you've ever grown zucchini, you know that there will always be plenty to share.) Dress gift packages from the garden to reflect the honesty of their origins. Vintage fruit baskets from country flea markets make excellent containers. Add a scrap of gingham or an antique tea towel as a liner. Even a faded bandanna knotted at the corners is ideal for passing along prized tomatoes. Or try kraft paper and twine to make a gift out of a bundle of sweet corn fresh from the garden or farmer's market.

Made for
the Shade

In the dog days of summer, nothing beats a shady retreat. If no trees are handy, build your own shelter with four bamboo poles and a sheet or an old tablecloth. Kids are experts at building forts from blankets, so make raising the roof a family affair. Add cool drinks, a good book, and lots of pillows, and you're set for an idyllic afternoon in your very own room with a view and a breeze.

In the calendar year, the summer solstice is a tipping point. Since winter, the days have marched steadily onward, each one gaining a little more precious light. On the solstice (around June 21), our part of the world is bathed with more daylight than on any other day of the year.

In Scandinavian countries the sun never really sets at this time of year, and the summer solstice is celebrated as a holiday called Midsummer with traditional dancing and singing.

SUMMER SOLSTICE

In fact, it has long been considered good luck to be married on Midsummer's day under the midnight sun.

Closer to home, we mark the solstice in quieter ways, if at all. By this time, we are truly in step with summer. On this longest day, when the sun seems to stand still in the sky, we are poised between the busyness of spring and the bounty of late summer and autumn. What better time to take a long, deep breath and appreciate nature's beauty in a whole new light.

A MIDSUMMER
NIGHT'S DREAM

*O*n midsummer evenings, the most captivating room in the house is just outside the front door. One of the charms of the porch is that it doesn't take much to transform it. Fill an urn with a bunch of just–picked hydrangeas and put down a cotton runner to dress up the space. Layer plenty of cushions on a swing or daybed to invite lounging and use plenty of candles to create just the right amount of lighting. Draping mosquito netting around the seating keeps pesky summer insects at bay and lends an air of romance.

WEEKEND GETAWAY

Listen closely and you can almost hear the waves. Even if the ocean is far away from your bedroom, it's still possible to create your own seashore retreat.

Select crisp, cool linens for the bed, slipcover chairs in summer whites, and mix an assortment of treasures from the sea with accessories in ocean hues. Here, draping frothy lengths of cotton over the bed creates a dreamy canopy and softens the lines of the bedposts. Collections of shells, sea glass, or bleached driftwood evoke the sea and can also be used to embellish a picture frame or mirror, planter, flea-market tray, or old wooden box.

Subtle reminders of sea and shore wash over the summer bedroom. On a weathered bedside cupboard, a tarnished silver serving dish holds an eclectic collection of shells. A unique coral candlestick and pearly button starfish hanging on the mirror extend the beachcomber theme.

OCEAN DREAMS Mementos from seashore visits can embellish the bedroom in endless ways. Small shells sewn onto a throw pillow, above, and strung onto a tassel, above right, add a touch of the sea in unexpected places. Wind chimes are easily made from small shells hung from fragments of driftwood. Larger scallop or oyster shells make perfect votive holders or bedside spots for jewelry or pocket change.

Beachcombers have an acquisitive eye for natural beauty—shells, sea glass, driftwood, colored pebbles. To draw more attention to subtle variations in color and form, group the same variety of sea shells together. Display the smallest or most fragile treasures, such as tiny cockle or scallop shells, in a shadow box. A Mediterranean-blue runner provides a beautiful backdrop for prized mementos casually displayed under glass. Even shell-inspired ornaments can nestle naturally among a mix of sea-washed shells. Vintage seaside photographs and postcards add a touch of nostalgia to the setting in keeping with the overall theme.

If you want a golden rule that will fit everything, this is it: Have nothing in your houses that you do not know to be useful or believe to be beautiful.

—William Morris

Sparklers and sweet corn, bare feet and barbecues, watermelon and water balloons, and a night sky illuminated by bursts and blooms. School's out, pools and beaches are open, and summer has hit full stride.

Somehow, Independence Day has a way of making every community feel like a small town. If only for a day, summer pastimes—horseshoes, sack races, badminton—are rediscovered and relished. While kids migrate from pool to playground and

FOURTH OF JULY

back again, neighbors chat across front porches as bunting and flags sway in the warm summer breeze.

As dusk falls, we gather family and friends on grassy terraces and settle on blankets to ooh and ahh at the annual fireworks spectacular. (Regardless of size or budget, it's always a spectacular.) And as showers of flickering stars spread across the dark sky and trail to the ground all around us, we realize that in summer, too, there's nothing quite like being home for the holidays.

All dressed up for the Fourth, the entry hall at River House offers an updated take on a classic theme. The faded reds and blues of the striped floor runner extend the patriotic palette to the floor while a vintage quilt pulls together an eye-catching welcome.

In honor of the Fourth, try a rendition of a star-spangled banister. Independence Day is the perfect opportunity to give star-shape ornaments that may only be brought out at Christmas a breath of fresh air. Hanging them from the hall ceiling, porch rail, mantel, or around a table will add a little twinkle to the celebration.

The summer dining room...

Open-air dining is a rite of the season, combining the casualness of a picnic with the convenience of a close-at-hand kitchen.

A patio party for the Fourth should be relaxed and easy for everyone—guests and host alike. Design the menu around fresh ingredients, simply prepared, to minimize time spent in the kitchen and maximize time spent with friends and family. Mixing elegant touches, such as vintage linens and glasses, with humble ones, such as storage-jar flower vases and mismatched cottage chairs, will set a comfortable tone. Hang clusters of stars over windows and doors, and, above all, fly the flag—or, better yet, fly lots of them.

Though it's not actually a law that watermelon be served at Fourth of July picnics, the grand old day wouldn't seem right without the heavyweight champ of summer fruits. Here, an antique enamel sink finds new life as the perfect watermelon cooler. Old galvanized washtubs make great ice chests, too.

The old red, white, and blue can take many forms on a tabletop steeped in nostalgia. A weathered old tricycle wears the winner's ribbon for things least likely to find as a centerpiece. With these colors as your theme, take the unlikely route to an entertaining table and be inspired by the ordinary. Here, vintage poker chips anchor a flag bouquet, and the soft blue glass of an old canning jar fits perfectly with the patriotic theme. Scour the garden for appropriate blooms—red geraniums and roses, blue cornflowers and larkspur, and white daisies and phlox.

Summer afternoon—
summer afternoon...
the two most beautiful
words in the
English language.

—Henry James

Why a parade?

Why a parade? Why fuss with such an old-fashioned tradition? It's a simple reason—perhaps it's mostly because we're proud. We're proud of our neighborhood, our town, our country, our ball team, our restored fire truck or rebuilt Model T Ford... even our shined-up vintage Schwinn. We're proud and we want the world—or at least our little piece of it—to know about it.

Regardless of why we do it, there's no parade quite like the small town Fourth of July parade. So there's no place we'd rather be on the Fourth than sitting on the curb of a flag-lined Main Street with family and friends, listening to the high school band and watching a corps of veterans, clowns, drill teams, dog walkers, and kids on bikes, and waving and cheering when we see familiar faces. The smaller and more ragtag the affair, the better. After all, enthusiasm and authenticity count for more than size and spectacle, and what better expression of this day is there than an old coaster-brake bike pulling a red wagon full of flag-waving toddlers?

PRESERVING LEAVES   HALLOWEEN   PUMPKIN CARVING

TRICK OR TREAT   CHILD'S THANKSGIVING   SEASONAL CORNUCOPIA

After the hazy chaos of summer, autumn arrives at River House full of crispness and clarity. The season of plenty—and plenty to do—autumn snaps us back on task. But if the chores are many, they are also sweetly satisfying. In the garden, late-ripening fruits and vegetables await the final harvest. Gardeners race against shortening days to gather peppers, summer-planted beans, spinach, and carrots. Safe from the first frost, a line of not-quite-ripe tomatoes marches across the kitchen windowsill.

FALL

Autumn means apples as crisp as an October morning. Empire and Braeburn, Jonathan and Macintosh, Golden Delicious and Gala—what isn't eaten straight off the tree is cored, peeled, and sliced, made into apple butter, pressed into cider, or cooked down to sauce. What Keats aptly called "the season of mellow fruitfulness" is the season for simmering pots on the stove, pies in the oven, canning jars in the cupboard, and trusted family recipes on the kitchen counter.

Fall isn't all chores, of course, at River House or surely in your own home. For every tidy pile of leaves raked, there's the fun of watching a giggling child play in the crunchy heap. Now is the time to savor every shining day and, with ruddy cheeks and cozy woolen sweaters, seize every opportunity to soak up the clear, bright light. Saturday-morning trips to the farmer's market are special, as the year's final harvest will soon be upon us. But, for now, farm stands and market bins overflow with an inspiring array of autumn produce. It's impossible to resist loading up with armfuls of apples and pears, pumpkins and squash, Indian corn, gourds, and sprigs of bittersweet.

There's much to do this time of year, to be sure. But there's even more to savor, to share, and to be thankful for. This season of abundance is also the season of gratitude, the season of family, and the season of gathering. During these golden days, we want nothing more than to be home again.

NO ORDINARY PANCAKE Autumn brings us to the very heart of baking season, and the delectable smells that drift from the kitchen have a way of transporting us back in time. Nothing, it seems, plays on the memory like the aroma of a dish enjoyed in childhood. For Dutch Americans in the upper Midwest, fall means pannekoeken, the Dutch equivalent of pancakes. This sweet, flaky popover can be made with any fruit filling, but our favorite employs a mix of oranges, cranberries, and apples spiced with cinnamon and sprinkled with toasted almonds. Our pannekoeken is best enjoyed with hot apple cider on a crisp fall night.

Autumn sometimes seems two seasons in one, the first spilling over with the richness of summer's ripened bounty and the other of simple quietude, reflection, and thankfulness. The transition is gradual, of course, and made all the easier if displays of treasures from the garden and farmer's market grace the sideboards and mantels of our homes. At this time of year, all the kitchen table at River House needs is an assortment of gourds and pumpkins, set off with sprigs of rosehips and bittersweet.

The aromas in the autumn kitchen are sweetly spiced and evocative: baking apples, roasting turkeys, and hearty soups and stews simmering all afternoon. Like the season itself, they promise pleasures both familiar and comforting.

Though pickings from the flower garden may be thin, the abundance of autumn produce affords endless opportunities to create captivating displays—apples and pears, and pumpkins, squash, and gourds in all shapes and sizes. These are nature's ornaments, after all. Pull them out of the kitchen, arrange them on a plate, heap them in a basket as a centerpiece, or simply line them up along a windowsill and let them glow.

Gather
Autumn Treasures

This season draws friends and neighbors to the house, and an indoor rug pulled out to the porch extends the welcome all the way to the front steps. Use the front porch, a naturally inviting area, as a place to preview decorating themes indoors. A bundle of corn-stalks or a display of golden-hued leaves will add a seasonal accent to the entrance. Here, a weathered old stepladder that's too wobbly for window washing serves as the perfect stage for jack-o'-lanterns to be.

SEASONAL GIFTS For a brief time, autumn leaves provide a rich source for crafting and decoration—they're beautiful, plentiful, and free for the taking. Left alone, the brilliant colors will quickly fade, but the leaves and their colors can be preserved.

Preserve leaves by pressing them in a hefty book for a few weeks. Use blotting paper on either side of the leaves to absorb moisture and protect the pages. Or seal leaves between two sheets of waxed paper using a warm iron (wrap the wax sheets in an old tea towel to keep your iron clean).

If you want to keep your leaves from drying out, put them in a mixture of one part glycerin to two parts water. After a few days, they can be removed from the solution and wiped dry.

Scatter preserved leaves around a centerpiece or weave the stems around a form or length of wire to make beautiful wreaths or garlands. Individual leaves can be framed, made into bookmarks, or used to personalize a seasonal card.

Nature sets the perfect spooky stage for Halloween. Chilly winds pull leaves from trees, leaving them skeleton bare and laying a creepy, crunchy carpet underfoot. Even the lights are dimmed early as daylight saving time ends before the haunting night. What better setting could there be for your own scary decorations?

Around this time, moms who knock down cobwebs the rest of the year spend hours artfully stretching fake webs over doorways and porches. Kids make eerie silhouettes and build newspaper-

HALLOWEEN

stuffed dummies with an attention to detail you dream they'd apply to their homework. Spooky cemeteries sprout in front yards all over the neighborhood.

Once the stage is set, an eager band of pint-size imposters begins a house-to-house performance. Pirates and princesses, mummies and mermaids, ghosts and goblins, witches... Halloween is that most glorious night when kids—even 50-year-old kids—get to indulge the fantasy of being a different character. No wonder we like it so much.

We're all for tradition, but orange isn't the only color for Halloween. The white-and-black scheme at River House lends a more sophisticated look to the season and evokes a ghostly, chilling effect. Try slipcovering a pair of chairs in black and white and designating one as the witch's seat. Against a stark white backdrop, vintage-style black cat silhouettes gain extra pop and loops of black rick rack add shivers to a line of antique silhouettes. Gather twigs from the yard and plant them in a black vase to make the perfect nesting spot for faux spiders and bats.

Finally, don't forget the ghostly white pumpkin. When spared from the carving knife, pumpkins usually last for weeks, and white pumpkins last even longer. Consider stenciling black letters or ghoulish faces on white pumpkins as an alternative to the traditional jack-o'-lantern.

There's no more traditional activity in fall than carving pumpkins. To plunge your hand into a freshly opened pumpkin is to plunge yourself right back into childhood. That cold, squishy mix of stringy pulp and slippery seeds still brings out a "Eeww!" just as surely as when we were six years old.

After scooping and scraping, the fun part begins… carving the perfect face. Nowadays, times have changed. The haphazard carving we gleefully practiced as kids has come a long way—and pumpkin carving has become something of an art form, complete with patterns, plans, and specialized tools. But why get too serious about such a silly custom? The toughest decision any carver should face is still the one we puzzled over as kids: scary face or funny face?

There's something altogether wholesome about pumpkins straight from the field. Lined up on porch steps and window sills, they make perfect natural decorations. But that's not all. With a little imagination, pumpkins provide perfect hiding spots or perches for spiders and bats, black cats and crows, scarecrows and ghosts, and other spooky creatures.

HOUSE OF TREATS For the perfect finishing touch, set a unique treat scene; after all, there's nothing scary about a plain mixing bowl full of candy. Here, treats are heaped inside a magical glass house whose door is just large enough to accommodate eager little hands. Ghostly pumpkin cutouts illuminated by candlelight cast spooky shadows on the scene, while black bottle-brush and tinsel trees add to the ambience.

To set the appropriate Halloween mood, dramatic lighting makes all the difference. Replace regular bulbs in porch fixtures with orange- or blue-tinted bulbs to cast an ominous glow—and just enough light to keep trick-or-treaters from toppling. On a wide front porch, place a collection of jack-o'-lanterns to light a path to a chill-inspiring haunted manor. Lanterns serve as handy footlights while maintaining the spooky mood.

Electric lights also offer a tantalizing range of possibilities. One surefire child pleaser is a strobe light, but be warned: With one of these on your porch trick-or-treaters may never want to move on to the next house. For other lighting options, snake a string of fairy lights through a scattering of dried leaves or put a black light and dry ice in shallow water at the bottom of a witch's kettle.

Whatever your lighting, leave a few dark corners on the way to the door. There's no telling what the big imaginations of small visitors will dream up to lurk in the shadows.

Kids love to decorate their own rooms, and Halloween is the perfect time to turn them loose. In other words, get out the orange and black construction paper and get out of the way. Add a paper witch's hat, spider, or tiny black bat to transform everyday companions, left. Cut out free-form paper ghosts and jack-o'-lanterns to decorate windows and doors. Set vintage-inspired characters on a tray sprinkled with candy corn or other mouthwatering treats. Finally, string Halloween lights along the bedstead to provide just enough illumination for spooky visitors and ghostly Halloween stories.

One little,
two little,
Three little witches
Fly over haystacks,
Fly over ditches,
Slide down the moon
Without any hitches,
Hey-ho!
Halloween's here!

trick
or
treat

To hear our grandparents tell it, there used to be a lot more trickery to "trick or treat" than there is nowadays. They love to talk about how Halloween was a night of soaping windows, egging houses, and tipping over outhouses.

Actually, the concept of trick-or-treating on Halloween most likely evolved from an ancient European custom called "souling." On November 2, All Souls Day, early Christians would walk from village to village, begging for "soul cakes," small biscuits with currants. The more cakes the beggars received, the more prayers they would say on behalf of the donor's ancestors.

For today's children, trick-or-treating is the combination of two natural passions— playing dress up and receiving massive amounts of candy. As caped and costumed children run from door to door, screams of delight rise up in response to generous givers. Shouts of "Wait up!" ring out to older siblings from the smallest members of the pack.

When the last doorbell is rung, there's nothing like an old-fashioned neighborhood Halloween party, complete with costume judging, bobbing for apples, sipping warm cider by the fire, and taking a few swings at a piñata. Thank goodness this tradition has evolved into a magical, candy-filled night.

Although the calendar still says it's fall, by the time Thanksgiving arrives the chill of winter has usually settled in. And we have done the same. Thanksgiving always draws us close to home and family. The day itself finds our homes dressed in full finery. Candles lit. Silver polished. Favorite fall centerpiece pulled from the cupboard. Linens pressed to crisp perfection. Amid the fall splendor, there's also a nod to winter's pending appearance. Drapes are drawn at night to fight the chill. There's a quilt on

THANKSGIVING

every bed and a warming fire crackling in the hearth.

Sandwiched between two spirited holidays, Thanksgiving is the quiet, reflective one. Ideally, it involves no major agendas or grand performances, save that of the cook. Rather, it gives us that rare relaxed moment to focus on the blessings we've received in the past year and to welcome family and close friends for the sheer pleasure of their company.

All of nature seems a still life in subdued and subtle tones in late autumn. ✌ Indoors at River House, pillows, throws, and quilts are changed to pick up fall's rich palette of amber, rust, copper, and gold and to enhance the seasonal displays. ✌ Although the colors are less vivid than in summer, the possibilities are endless. Consider gourds in all shapes and sizes, hydrangeas, crab apples, rosehips, feathery wild grasses, sumac, and bittersweet. Put them in your favorite wicker container or amber glass vase, tuck them into wall pockets, or elevate them on a simple decorative pedestal—with these arrangements there's no need to water.

Study nature,
love nature,
stay close to nature.
It will never
fail you.
—Frank Lloyd Wright

Timeless tradition and contemporary embellishments are equally at home on a well-dressed Thanksgiving table. But always try to include some personal touches amid all the traditional trappings. Unexpected details, such as leaves looped over chair backs or place cards tucked into dried artichokes, add individual style. Use a multitiered arrangement of seasonal fruits—figs, grapes, pomegranates, pears, and persimmons—to add fall color to the tabletop.

Don't forget to decorate the mantel for the occasion: a pair of cinnamon-colored candles in hurricane lamps can anchor a group of pumpkins and gourds set among bittersweet, Chinese lanterns, and autumn leaves.

CARAMEL APPLES Too good to eat only at Halloween, caramel apples can become a new Thanksgiving tradition—a festive alternative to apple pie. And with a few simple twists, a plain-Jane apple can turn into a tempting treat of your own creation. While the caramel is still warm, roll coated apples through finely chopped toasted pecans, toasted coconut, or crunched-up, chocolate-coated toffee bars. If toppings won't stick, warm the caramel apples in the microwave—but only for a few seconds. Too much time will cause the caramel to slide off the apple.

If a caramel coating isn't decadent enough, dip refrigerator-chilled caramel apples halfway into a pan of melted chocolate. You can even go all out and dip once more into candy sprinkles.

TRADITIONS

Be thankful for the kids' Thanksgiving table. For generations, this clever tradition has given kids the thrill of their very own table while allowing grown-ups to enjoy the big meal in relative peace.

In a casual setting of mix-and-match chairs and benches, delight and surprise the group by adding a few unexpected treats. Welcome them with Pilgrim-style shoe buckles made of black construction paper, which serve as name cards and napkin rings. Equip the table with a container of crayons and a runner made from the morning newspaper for them to decorate—if you plan a few days ahead, you can use the Sunday funnies. Decorate the area with images of turkeys, Pilgrims, and other symbols of the day, and include some Thanksgiving-themed playing cards and books on the table to remind them how this holiday came to be. With all the fun they'll be having at the kiddie table, adults may request a seat here for next year's gathering.

Artful abundance should be the dominant decorating theme throughout the house at Thanksgiving. Transform an antique secretary into an overflowing buffet with russet- and cream-colored transferware and a cornucopia of autumn produce. On a side table, a richly colored collection of gourds provides a counterpoint to a simple Indian figure. Add sprigs of bittersweet and a tiny nesting bird for a sweet surprise amid a display of silver cups. Continuing the nature theme, nest a creamy ceramic pumpkin on a pedestal lined with brightly colored leaves.

Thanksgiving Day comes, by statute, once a year; to the honest man it comes as frequently as the heart of gratitude will allow.

—Edward Sandford Martin

Simply abundant. The cornucopia, spilling over with the fruits of harvest, reigns as an icon of autumn. Derived from the Latin for "horn of plenty," this basket is the most traditional of Thanksgiving centerpieces. Classically, it overflows with fruits, vegetables, gourds, and Indian corn. But don't confine this iconic embellishment to the dining table. Cornucopias are warm, welcoming arrangements in a front hallway or guest bedroom or on a broad kitchen window sill. Smaller versions—loaded perhaps with cookies, jams, chocolates, teas, or coffees—make much-appreciated gifts.

Although the tradition of the cornucopia is ancient, its meaning is still relevant today. Because it symbolizes the bounty of life, it can help remind us of the bounty and blessings we've received throughout the year. As a modern-day take on the horn of plenty, ask guests around the Thanksgiving table to write down something they're thankful for and tuck the notes into a cornucopia centerpiece. Before enjoying dinner, read the notes aloud to give thanks.

CHRISTMAS WELCOME   GIFT GIVING   TREE TRIMMING

CHRISTMAS STOCKINGS   NEW YEAR'S EVE   VALENTINE'S DAY

Winter arrives early in our part of the country, and that suits us fine. By the time the first flurries fly, River House is ready. Snugged up tight against the cold, with firewood stacked high and outdoor furniture stashed away for the season, the house stands steadfast to face winter for almost the 150th time.

In the surrounding woods, deciduous trees have completed their cycle from bud to blossom, green leaf to gold, and have gone dormant again. Now is the evergreen's time to shine. A walk

among our trees and a bit of seasonal pruning supplies a basketful of fir and pine—soon to become wreaths and garlands. As we make our rounds, the snow-blanketed stillness is interrupted only by the chattering of squirrels and the chirping of winter songbirds. The rhythm of nature has slowed to a muffled beat.

Inside River House, it's a different story. Within its white-washed clapboard walls, a welcoming warmth radiates from every room as preparations are made for the holiday season ahead.

The fire crackles in the hearth and the air itself is electric with anticipation. This is it—the season we look forward to all year. We're more than just enthusiasts. We're unabashed Christmas fanatics, and dressing the house in its Christmas finery is the highlight of our year.

We are believers in tradition, but not mired in it. Yes, the same treasured ornaments see use every year, but in new ways and unexpected combinations. Each room brings a new opportunity to experiment with colors, textures, and forms. We think beyond the tree and mantel—embellishing mirrors and windows, hallway lights and porch rails. At this time of year, we blend old with new, formal with frivolous, and the tarnished with the twinkling.

So welcome, welcome to winter—season of chilled air, warm laughter, and snowfalls that soften the world around us. Welcome to chubby snowmen with stick arms, to kettles whistling on the stove, and to mittens drying on the radiator. Welcome, at last, to the season of stuffed stockings, wreaths on the door, and pretty packages. Welcome Christmas thrill and New Year's cheer. Come frost, ice, or snow, winter is warmly welcomed here.

SETTING A
SEASONAL STAGE

Woven among antique frames, a beaded glass garland links generations of family photographs. Whether they're made of paper, vintage beads, cranberries, pinecones, or fresh greenery, think of hanging garlands around the house before Christmas decorations proper go up. Drape them around windows or doorways, loop them along mantels or bookshelves. For a more luxurious look, layer two or more together.

At River House, we begin decorating early. As nature becomes dormant and outdoor colors more muted, there's something energizing and exciting about introducing color and life inside. To begin, the changes are gradual: A wreath is hung on the front door, extra candles are put on the mantel, a garland of evergreens is hung on the staircase.

In the kitchen, the sideboard gets a generous bedding of fir boughs as a foundation for fresh fruits and a sprinkling of jewellike ornaments. A wrapping of gold bullion wire dresses up the simple taper candles and adds a touch of sparkle to the natural arrangement.

Room by room, go beyond tradition. The palette of Christmas is not fixed, so an easy way to get a fresh look is by using colors other than red and green. Keep the mix harmonious by choosing a single palette for each room: snowy whites and creams for one setting, rich purples and golds for another.

Dripping with glimmering silvers, soft greens, and icy-blues, this dazzling chandelier shimmers like a frozen waterfall. This wintry cascade of colors sets the tone for the entire room.

Coordinated by color and clustered for increased effect, these otherwise ordinary ornaments are guaranteed to garner a second look. The clear glass urns and opaque ornaments echo the look of the chandelier that establishes the room's decorating scheme.

FREE YOUR ORNAMENTS Think beyond the tree and use simple ornaments in unexpected ways to add notes of surprise in each room. Ornaments are ideal for seasonal tablescapes or for adding a spirited splash to window treatments, sills, or even to (low-traffic) doorknobs. Double your decorating fun by hanging several colored baubles from a ribbon in front of a mirror. Nestle others among potted plants, pile them up in fruit bowls, or let them sparkle amid a collection of votive candles. Just don't forget to save some for the tree!

ALL THAT
GLITTERS

In our minds, memories, and hearts, Christmas holds a place all its own. It has its own language: When but in December do you hear the words sugarplum, tinsel, feather tree, or wassail? And, of course, it has its own aromas, unchanged by the decades. Years melt away when the balsam scent of a fir tree first fills our homes. Suddenly, we are six years old again, filled with excitement, peeking through banisters, looking for Santa.

For many of us, these memories are inextricably tied to the

trimmings and decorations of the season. A fragile antique crèche is placed in the same spot each year. The simple act of opening a box of treasured ornaments can be a homecoming.

Christmas traditions—and even decorations—hold remarkable power. They connect us to the past, but their brightness and spirit also help us celebrate the present. Decorated for Christmas, a home seems more a home somehow. And gathered together for Christmas, a family seems more a family.

The cheer starts here. Adorned with king-size wreaths and swags of garland, the front entrance to River House projects the warmest of greetings. The use of wreaths and garlands as Christmas décor predates the advent of Christmas trees by centuries. In many European cultures, evergreen branches in the home served as a welcome sign of life during cold, bleak winters. The first recorded use of the Advent wreath dates to sixteenth century Germany. Then, as now, Advent wreaths held four candles that were lighted, one per week, throughout the month leading up to Christmas.

Today, wreaths are more popular than ever, with adaptations that make them appropriate for every season: fresh flowers in spring or summer, berries or foliage in fall, pine cones or even a colorful mix of favorite Christmas ornaments in winter. Still, there is something refreshingly honest and timeless about a simple evergreen wreath dotted with holly berries. Well before a visitor sets foot inside, a Christmas wreath on the door makes it clear that this is truly a home for the holidays.

LET HEAVEN
AND NATURE
SING!

A red-and-gold theme stands out against the snowy-white backdrop of the entrance hall, greeting friends and family alike. Bare winter branches take on a supporting role as a perfect framework for a jubilant mix of scarlet baubles and glittering gold stars. The palette continues in the fragrant paper-whites, carpet of red poinsettias, and clear glass urn filled with crimson cranberries. Hanging cones decorate the newel post at the foot of the stairs. Leading the eye up the staircase, an evergreen swag interlaced with a cranberry-red garland and a sprinkling of gold stars ensures an enchanted trip to bed.

Christmas is the season for kindling the fire of hospitality in the hall, the genial flame of charity in the heart.

—Washington Irving

Setting the right atmosphere is key to making card writing a true pleasure. Cue up your favorite Christmas music, find a comfy seat, surround yourself with cherished holiday decorations, and let the well-wishing words flow. Everyone likes little surprises at this time of year, so put something extra in the envelope. Simple gold stars add a dash of sparkle; a child's drawing or paper angel would also personalize your message.

CHRISTMAS CARD WREATH Some cards are too beautiful—or too meaningful—to throw away or keep hidden in a drawer. This year's cards can be hung from ribbons or strung from long, colored cords across a mantel or window, and the most precious cards from Christmases past can be displayed on a wire card holder. Cherished messages from family and friends, handmade gift tags, even cherished holiday photographs can all take their place around this wreath. Hung from a ribbon, it forms a treasured keepsake that's updated with fresh memories every year.

Better to give than to receive? As kids, we laughed at that

old notion, but now…well, there's a reason we call such sayings "truisms." Few things are more satisfying than thinking of—and tracking down—the perfect gift for someone on your list. To present the unexpected and inspired gift brings a level of excitement that approaches that feeling we used to have as children, anticipating Santa's arrival.

Of course, finding the perfect gift is just the beginning. Presentation counts—an imaginative wrapping or gift tag makes the contents all the more special. To the vast array of options available in stores, you can add a truly endless list of creative alternatives. Vintage sheet music, old maps, comics or newspapers, or scraps of old wallpaper can all be repurposed for wrapping. Access to a color printer or copying machine opens up new possibilities. Dress up kraft paper by stamping with a purchased or homemade stamp— metallic inks look particularly festive. Choose complementary ribbon and tie an appropriate add-on to the top of the package—an ornament, a sprig of evergreen, holly, or ivy, or a tiny snapshot of the lucky recipient.

Color trends come and go, but a Christmas tree always looks well dressed in a classic red, gold, and green ensemble. On our entryway tree, big, gold-glittered stars coordinate with more delicate embellishments like clustered painted glass bells and finely detailed Father Christmas figurines. A garland of red and gold beads draped over the boughs pulls the outfit together and lends an air of old-fashioned elegance to this stately grand dame.

As family traditions go, this one is personal.

A Christmas tree is more than just a seasonal decoration—it is truly a family time capsule. And to trim a tree with your family is to journey into memories of Christmases past. Each ornament has its story, and each has the capacity to transport us through time. A simple silver bell that marks your child's first Christmas. A sloppy but sincere salt-dough star that hearkens to third-grade art class. A fine, fragile bird that has been passed down through careful hands.

If a tree-trimming party isn't already a tradition in your home, it may be an activity whose time has come. Invite friends—especially those away from their own family—for an evening dedicated to decking out the tree. You'll be surprised by how refreshing a little outside inspiration can be, and nothing spurs so many fond memories as the shared act of trimming a tree. At night's end, send your guests home with a gift basket of ornaments for their own tree.

As the distinctive aromas of nutmeg, cinnamon, ginger, and clove fill the house, there can be no doubt that the holiday baking season is upon us. Every family has its baking traditions, and those surrounding Christmas cookies are particularly revered.

Baking and decorating Christmas cookies with kids is a real delight, and it's a great way to pass the time between sled runs. Cookie-cutter cookies are the classic kid pleaser, as they involve the triple thrill of rolling dough, cutting forms, and decorating. Just be sure you have plenty of colored sugar, sprinkles, and silver dragées on hand—and, of course, a complete palette of frosting colors.

GINGERBREAD HOUSE The ultimate edible centerpiece is also the perfect kids' holiday kitchen project. Originally inspired by the Brothers Grimm fairy tale, "Hansel and Gretel," gingerbread houses became a craze in Germany in the early nineteenth century. Today, the classic gingerbread house is still the stuff of childhood dreams. Kits are widely available for those who want to keep construction time to a minimum and get right to the decorating. A few tips and tricks: Shake shredded coconut in a baggie with green food coloring to make grass. Crisped rice and marshmallow treats dyed green make great shrubs (dot with Red Hots candy for holly bushes). Melt butterscotch discs for micalike windows. Small pretzel sticks make nice fences, and old-fashioned red-and-white candy canes make perfect porch and light posts. When finished, dust with powdered sugar to add a light layer of fresh snow to the cozy cottage.

Decorating for the holidays sweetens every room in the house, but it's often most intricate in the kitchen. This is no time for drudgery. Keep recipes simple and you'll leave plenty of time for the fun parts. Shortbread, Spritz, gingerbread, and sugar cookies are all easily prepared and perfect candidates for decorating. Allow kids lots of artistic freedom and give the finished products out at neighborhood cookie exchanges, holiday parties, or tree-trimming galas. And, don't forget to let them decorate a special cookie for Santa on Christmas Eve.

BAKE A DAY OF IT

Setting up a small tree in the kids' room gives them a decorating project all their own and serves as a great place to show off favorite ornaments, homemade or otherwise. ❧ Hung in the window, an Advent calendar made from flashcards entices little hands with a fresh ornament each day. ❧ Dressing sock monkeys for the season doesn't require advanced sewing skills, especially if you use felt or colored construction paper. ❧ Many people of Scandinavian and eastern European descent celebrate St. Nicholas Eve (December 5), when shoes left by the bedroom door are filled with sweets, chocolate coins, or small toys.

At Christmas play
and make good cheer,
for Christmas comes
but once a year.
—Thomas Tusser

Christmas is a time not only to bring the outdoors in but also to take the indoors out. Placing a tree on the porch carries the spirit of the season outside and is an inviting welcome to guests.

From the plain burlap skirt to the twisted-twig bird's nest perched near its top, everything on this tree is inspired by woodlands and was chosen to be in harmony with the winter setting. Painted pinecone ornaments look right at home on its boughs, and feathers and blown-glass birds perch in every nook. Bird Christmas tree ornaments have long carried religious and secular symbolism: According to old German custom, finding a bird's nest on a tree will bring good fortune throughout the coming year.

Nature's own ornaments—pinecones, acorns, icicles, mushrooms, and bird nests— have inspired ornament makers for centuries. Real pinecones were often left on the balsam fir trees that European families brought into their homes for Christmas. Considered symbols of eternity and motherhood, they were among the first ornaments designed by German glassblowers in the mid- nineteenth century.

NATURE'S GIFTS

*I*t's hard to keep kids' excitement from bubbling over on this long-awaited night, but setting a tradition of reading a Christmas story is a wonderful way to calm fidgety little ones and still maintain the spirit of the evening. It's hard work going up and down chimneys all night, so don't forget to leave Santa a snack for his efforts. Milk and cookies go down best with a handwritten note from the children of the house.

A welcome hush seems to fall over River House on Christmas Eve. The rush of shopping, baking, wrapping, and writing is finally over. For most people, this is a night reserved for family, with church services, a festive dinner, and perhaps carols around the fire. For children, the long wait is nearly over. In the hours before bedtime, they'll likely trace the course from stockings to Christmas tree countless times, imagining Santa's arrival with almost unbearable anticipation. The tree looms large to children—at first a friendly stranger in the room, it quickly becomes a comforting presence and a symbol of pure joy.

Hung by the chimney with care, stockings are an essential part of Christmas lore and décor. But how did they end up there in the first place? The tradition of hanging stockings most likely began with Saint Nicholas, many centuries before Clement C. Moore included the now-familiar phrase in his poem, *A Visit From St. Nicholas* (widely known as *The Night Before Christmas*). Saint Nicholas is said to have thrown coins down the chimneys of peasants on Christmas Eve so that the next morning, the poor but good-hearted would find their stockings weighted with gold.

The mantel is still a favorite place for stockings, but if you'd rather keep the hearth clear for Santa, consider hanging stockings from the staircase banister or children's bedposts. The front door is a great spot for a stocking stuffed with greenery or welcome-home candy canes. Stockings look best when clustered en masse, mixed and matched. Consider adding one or two containing small toys and gifts to be donated to charity—a great lesson for kids about the true spirit of Christmas. And don't forget to include stockings for the pampered pets in the house. Santa is known to have a soft spot for four-legged friends.

Moments of stillness and serenity

are much sought at Christmas but often hard to come by. Our tablescapes illustrate how gathering a few well-chosen and well-placed elements can create a simple ode to the quiet joys of the season. When decorating with your favorite mementos, try to explore the entire spectrum of holiday moods, from festive and fun to sincere and quiet.

Changing the presentation of your most familiar holiday scenes gives them new life. Opposite, a traditional crèche gains added resonance under a cloche. Cloches, or bell jars, originally used to protect plants from cold weather, have a contrary effect in decorating. They seem to freeze a moment in time, and the scenes within them become compelling still lifes.

NEW YEAR'S EVE

Surrounded by cherished friends…what better way to ring out the old year and ring in the new?

This night is made for indulgences—for our guests and for ourselves. From gifts on each chair to lavishly layered table settings, everything in this room communicates a message of generosity and graciousness.

Rooms lit by candlelight take on a magical quality. If candles alone are insufficient, small sidelights will provide enough illumination without breaking the dreamy spell.

Though the look is certainly "special occasion," our New Year's room setting is far from imposing. Winsome touches—twinkling stars hung from the real candle chandelier and a refreshingly informal centerpiece of paperwhites—keep the spirit lively and light.

NEW YEAR'S WISHES For a lively New Year's table conversation, ask guests to share their resolutions for the coming year. Write them down and tuck them away so they can be retrieved before next year's celebration. Alternatively, have guests write down their wishes for the New Year. When all are finished, collect the wishes and toss them into the fire. The rising smoke will carry the wishes to the heavens.

Valentine's Day provides a touch of cheer and color when we need it most. Well before the spring thaw, this day of love has an uncanny way of warming hearts. The feast day of St. Valentine has been part of religious celebrations since the fifth century, and long before that, the Romans held a mid-February celebration that paired young couples. But Valentine's Day as we know it—a day dedicated to expressions of love and affection—dates to seventeenth-century Britain.

The traditional trappings—hearts and roses and chocolates—are enduring fixtures. But why not bake a batch of your loved one's favorite cookies? Or give a first edition of a favorite book or put together a personalized photo album of a recent vacation? Make it a family occasion: Kids love Valentine's Day—and not just because of the candy. It's the perfect occasion for budding artists and craftsy kids to create frilly, glittery cards and decorations. After all, it's been nearly two months since Christmas. Doesn't the house deserve a colorful holiday makeover?

A Glimpse
of Spring

CREDITS

Thank you to the many incredibly talented and wonderful people who made CELEBRATING HOME a reality, especially writer Patrick Regan, photographer Susan Gentry McWhinney, and stylist Jane Dagmi.

A very special thanks to the Midwest team of Jeff Wilson, Ingrid Liss, Margo Tantau, Beth Lorentz, Shelli Lissick, Chris Tkachuck, Brent Thomas, Sara Dewanz, Brian Walker and Victoria McGuire for their time, talents and dedication to creating CELEBRATING HOME. Several artists' works are featured in the book, and we especially thank Wendy Addison, Nicol Sayre and Penny McAllister for their creations. We also appreciate and thank others who helped out on the project, including Aaron Parker, photographer, and Lori Hellander and Linda Cogger, photo stylists. And finally, thanks to the many other employees of Midwest and their family members for giving of their gardens, their closets, their children and their time.

A special debt of thanks to those who restored and furnished the Seasons of Cannon Falls River House: Architect, Laurel Ulland, Domain Architecture & Design; Contractor, Mark Mueller-Dahl, Mueller-Dahl Interiors; Project Manager, Dennis Kalow; Interior Designers, John and Carol Smallwood; Interior Decorator, Linda Schneewind; Landscape Designers, Tom Nelson, Woodsend, and Thomas Kerby, Landform.

RESOURCES

SEASONS OF CANNON FALLS®
SEASONAL & HOLIDAY ACCESSORIES

MIDWEST
32057 64th Avenue
Cannon Falls, Minnesota 55009
800-776-2075 corporate headquarters
800-337-3335 consumer line
www.seasonsonline.com

Seasons of Cannon Falls holiday and seasonal decorative products are available for purchase through specialty retailers, department stores, mail order and online sources throughout the United States. To locate a retailer near you, visit www.seasonsonline.com.

Thank you to the following retailers, antique dealers and manufacturers for their contributions to this book.

ANTIQUE SHOPS

COUNTRY SIDE ANTIQUE MALL
Chuck Drometer & the many other dealers
31752 65th Avenue
Cannon Falls, Minnesota 55009
507-263-0352
www.csamantiques.com
Vintage tableware, linens, primitives and pottery.

HAUPT ANTIEK
Deb Haupt & the many other dealers
14690 South Robert Trail
Rosemont, Minnesota 55068
651-329-3871
www.hauptantiek.com
Primitives, vintage cottage and seasonal antiques.

HUNT & GATHER
Kristi Stratton & the many other dealers
4944 Xerxes Avenue South
Minneapolis, Minnesota 55410
612-455-0250
Primitives, vintage fabrics, industrial chic, and jewelry.

THE MARKET
Anastasia Balfany
421 Division Street South
Northfield, Minnesota 55057
507-663-7733
www.themarket.us
Sophisticated classical antiques.

THORA MAE'S ANTIQUES
Laurie Sobottka & the many other dealers
31265 Country 24 Blvd
Cannon Falls, Minnesota 55009
507-263-2073
Vintage glassware, linens, and pottery.

VINTAGE FABRICS & ETC.
Margaret Meier
3500 C N.E. 11th Avenue
Oakland Park, Florida 33334
954-564-4392
Vintage linens and textiles.

HOME ACCESSORIES

DIGS
Linda Schneewind
310 Division Street South
Northfield, Minnesota 55057
507-664-9140
Home furnishings, upholstery, accessories and details.

FARIBAULT WOOLEN MILLS
Gale Moesler
1500 NW 2nd Avenue
Faribault, Minnesota 55021
800-533-0444
www.faribaultmills.com
Colorful and cozy blankets.

RED & WHITE KITCHEN COMPANY
P.O. Box 619
Mount Kisco, New York 10549
www.redandwhitekitchen.com
Minnesota sack cloth linens used to make pillows (page 69).

WAVERLY FABRICS
800-423-5881
www.waverly.com
*Stripes, florals and rich damask fabrics (Sweet Violets
Vintage/blush #662490 chair pad fabric, page 30;
Sussex/buttercream #665651 oversized bolster, page 40;
Randolph Check/red #64821 chair pad, pages 48, 49;
Paisley Sheer/ivory #615331 bed canopy, page 60; and
Dotted Swiss tablecloth, pages 30, 31).*

First published in the United States in 2005
by Midwest of Cannon Falls,
32057 64th Avenue,
Cannon Falls, Minnesota 55009

First Edition
ISBN 0-9763837-6-4
Library of Congress Control Number 2005927660

PRODUCED BY SMALLWOOD & STEWART, INC.,
NEW YORK CITY
PHOTOGRAPHY BY SUSAN GENTRY MCWHINNEY
STYLING BY JANE DAGMI
TEXT BY PATRICK REGAN
DESIGNED BY ALEXIS SIROC

Printed in Singapore
1 2 3 4 5 6 7 8 / 08 07 06 05 04 03 02 01